THE
MINGLING
OF
SOULS

GOD'S DESIGN FOR LOVE, MARRIAGE, SEX & REDEMPTION

MATT CHANDLER
WITH JIM GRIBNITZ

1st edition 2015

Published by

3405 Milton Avenue, Suite 207
Dallas, TX 75205

Printed in the United States

TABLE OF CONTENTS

ACKNOWLEDGMENTS

First of all, I'd like to thank Jim Gribnitz for his writing and passion for crafting questions that lead to great conversations.

The Village Church—especially the media and communications team—made this series happen, and I am very grateful for their expertise, support, and friendship.

We could never have accomplished this curriculum without the help of:

Matt Coleman, Grant Wakefield, and the entire *Unblind Productions team*
Shatrine Krake and Krake Designs
Drew Rodgers with Livingstone Designs
Sue Ann Reynolds with Round Tu-It
David C Cook and team

About Jim Gribnitz

This is the sixth curriculum book Jim has written for The Hub. He has been a pastor on staff at large churches for more than fifteen years in the Dallas area. He has an MBA in international business and a master's and doctorate from Dallas Seminary. Jim is a sought-after speaker and conference leader, especially for helping parents and teens understand the influence of technology and media on the next generation. He lives in Dallas with his wife, Nikki, and their three children.

STUDY TIPS

BEFORE YOU GO ANY FURTHER ... READ THIS!

If you are a small group leader, thanks for taking the opportunity to shepherd others along the way. And if you are using this series for personal study, get ready for a life-changing experience you will want to share with others!

Here are a few tips as you start the series:

• This study was designed with small groups in mind. So put a small group together and get started.
• The series is also perfect for individuals or couples who are looking for ways to deepen their devotions or to find practical ways to apply the timeless truths of Scripture.
• *The Mingling of Souls* is designed to be used as either a twelve-week or a six-week study. Each DVD session is approximately thirty minutes. The sessions are designed to be used as follows: watch each session and then discuss the questions in the study guide. Depending on the length of your meeting, you can watch two sessions at a time in order to shorten *The Mingling of Souls* to a six-week series.

A WORD TO SMALL GROUP LEADERS

Special Note: Take a moment to go to the Behind the Book feature (page 79). This is a quick overview that will give you the who, what, when, where, and why of the Song of Solomon. There is no separate leader's guide. Leaders are facilitators of the material.

Before each session we encourage leaders to:

• Pray – ask the Lord for guidance on how to lead the members in your group. Pray that he will show you ways to stimulate genuine, dynamic, and open communication.
• Preview – it will be very beneficial for you to watch the session before you share it with your group. You will notice the key points from each session and will be able to better facilitate the discussion questions within your group.
• Prepare – a small group will only go as deep and be as transparent as the leader. If a leader or facilitator is not willing to get personal, then the group will float on the surface. Let God speak through your own struggles and weaknesses.

ABOUT THE AUTHOR

Matt Chandler serves as Lead Pastor of Teaching at The Village Church in the Dallas/Fort Worth metroplex. He came to The Village in December 2002 and describes his tenure as a replanting effort where he was involved in changing the theological and philosophical culture of the congregation. The church has witnessed a tremendous response growing from 160 people to over 13,000, with campuses in Flower Mound, Dallas, Denton, Plano, and Fort Worth.

Matt is currently involved in church planting efforts both locally and internationally through The Village and various strategic partnerships. He serves as president of Acts 29, a worldwide church-planting organization. Over the last ten years, Acts 29 has emerged from a small band of brothers to nearly five hundred churches in the United States and around the world.

Beyond speaking at conferences throughout the world, Matt has also written four books: *The Explicit Gospel*, published in April 2012; *Creature of the Word*, released in October 2012; *To Live Is Christ to Die Is Gain*, released in September 2013; and *Recovering Redemption*, released in May 2014. His greatest joy outside of Jesus is being married to Lauren and being a dad to their three children, Audrey, Reid, and Norah.

ONE

LET THE MINGLING BEGIN

Gotta love family.

One of the most popular things that couples or singles especially say to me in both coun-seling situations and casual conversations is something about how their family (or the family of their spouse or fiancé) is flat-out messed up. The bad news is that they prob-ably are to some degree, but the good news is that they are not alone. Families are...ya know...families.

The generic conversation usually goes something like this:
Them: My family has problem X.
Me: What happens when you bring that up with them to talk about?
Them: Ooooohhhhh...We don't talk about it. That's not what we do in my family.

I have to be honest that I have never understood why people who love each other would have certain topics that are off-limits. The standing rule in my family with my wife and kids is that anything and everything is on the table—especially things of great importance. We are open and honest with one another. That is just who we are.

Therefore, families that keep dancing around certain topics baffle me. I still rack my brain wondering: *Why do so many families, singles, parents, and couples avoid talking about deeply relational issues such as sex? Why is that "off the table"? Does it make us too squeamish? Does it make us blush? Is it inappropriate?*

The problem with being content to avoid that topic is that the God who created us (and sex) talks about it all the time. In fact, he has intentionally preserved certain sacred writ-ings for a few thousand years that talked about all sorts of important things. Deeply rela-tional issues that we tend to make private matters.

Love. Dating. Romance. Sex.

More than just these, he talked about relationships. What does a *real* relationship look like? Not the garbage we see on TV with a man and woman (or two men or two women) who don't know how to forgive, can't carry on an intimate conversation, and just jumps into the sack for inconsequential sex with someone he or she just met because they are cute...But a *real* relationship.

Something with depth. Something with oomph. Something that matters. Something that fulfills.

These are important things to talk about, and you should know that God will not blush as he talks about this.

Neither should we.

SCRIPTURE

GENESIS 1—3
Creation of Man & Woman: 1:26-31

1:26Then God said, "Let us make mankind in our image, in our likeness, so that they may rule over the fish in the sea and the birds in the sky, over the livestock and all the wild animals, and over all the creatures that move along the ground."

27So God created mankind in his own image, in the image of God he created them; male and female he created them.

28God blessed them and said to them, "Be fruitful and increase in number; fill the earth and subdue it. Rule over the fish in the sea and the birds in the sky and over every living creature that moves on the ground."

29Then God said, "I give you every seed-bearing plant on the face of the whole earth and every tree that has fruit with seed in it. They will be yours for food. 30And to all the beasts of the earth and all the birds in the sky and all the creatures that move along the ground—everything that has the breath of life in it—I give every green plant for food." And it was so.

31God saw all that he had made, and it was very good. And there was evening, and there was morning—the sixth day.

Creation of Man & Woman: 2:18-25

2:18The Lord God said, "It is not good for the man to be alone. I will make a helper suitable for him."

19Now the Lord God had formed out of the ground all the wild animals and all the birds in the sky. He brought them to the man to see what he would name them; and whatever the man called each living creature, that was its name. 20So the man gave names to all the livestock, the birds in the sky and all the wild animals.

But for Adam no suitable helper was found. 21So the Lord God caused the man to fall into a deep sleep; and while he was sleeping, he took one of the man's ribs and then closed up the place with flesh. 22Then the Lord God made a woman from the rib he had taken out of the man, and he brought her to the man.

SCRIPTURE

²³The man said, "This is now bone of my bones and flesh of my flesh; she shall be called 'woman,' for she was taken out of man."

²⁴That is why a man leaves his father and mother and is united to his wife, and they become one flesh.

²⁵Adam and his wife were both naked, and they felt no shame.

Fall: 3:1–24

³ᐟ¹Now the serpent was more crafty than any of the wild animals the Lord God had made. He said to the woman, "Did God really say, 'You must not eat from any tree in the garden'?"

²The woman said to the serpent, "We may eat fruit from the trees in the garden, ³but God did say, 'You must not eat fruit from the tree that is in the middle of the garden, and you must not touch it, or you will die.'"

⁴"You will not certainly die," the serpent said to the woman.

⁵"For God knows that when you eat from it your eyes will be opened, and you will be like God, knowing good and evil."

⁶When the woman saw that the fruit of the tree was good for food and pleasing to the eye, and also desirable for gaining wisdom, she took some and ate it. She also gave some to her husband, who was with her, and he ate it. ⁷Then the eyes of both of them were opened, and they realized they were naked; so they sewed fig leaves together and made coverings for themselves. ⁸Then the man and his wife heard the sound of the Lord God as he was walking in the garden in the cool of the day, and they hid from the Lord God among the trees of the garden. ⁹But the Lord God called to the man, "Where are you?" ¹⁰He answered, "I heard you in the garden, and I was afraid because I was naked; so I hid." ¹¹And he said, "Who told you that you were naked? Have you eaten from the tree that I commanded you not to eat from?" ¹²The man said, "The woman you put here with me—she gave me some fruit from the tree, and I ate it." ¹³Then the Lord God said to the woman, "What is this you have done?" The woman said, "The serpent deceived me, and I ate."

SCRIPTURE

¹⁴So the Lord God said to the serpent, "Because you have done this, "Cursed are you above all livestock and all wild animals! You will crawl on your belly and you will eat dust all the days of your life.

¹⁵And I will put enmity between you and the woman, and between your offspring and hers; he will crush your head, and you will strike his heel."

¹⁶ To the woman he said, "I will make your pains in childbearing very severe; with painful labor you will give birth to children. Your desire will be for your husband, and he will rule over you."

¹⁷To Adam he said, "Because you listened to your wife and ate fruit from the tree about which I commanded you, 'You must not eat from it,' cursed is the ground because of you; through painful toil you will eat food from it all the days of your life.

¹⁸It will produce thorns and thistles for you, and you will eat the plants of the field.

¹⁹By the sweat of your brow you will eat your food until you return to the ground, since from it you were taken; for dust you are and to dust you will return."

²⁰Adam named his wife Eve, because she would become the mother of all the living.

²¹The Lord God made garments of skin for Adam and his wife and clothed them. ²²And the Lord God said, "The man has now become like one of us, knowing good and evil. He must not be allowed to reach out his hand and take also from the tree of life and eat, and live forever." ²³So the Lord God banished him from the Garden of Eden to work the ground from which he had been taken. ²⁴After he drove the man out, he placed on the east side of the Garden of Eden cherubim and a flaming sword flashing back and forth to guard the way to the tree of life.

QUESTIONS

There are wounds that get revealed as we seek intimate relationships that reveal our deep need for the Lord.

Matt mentions that, at the time these messages were recorded, on Amazon there were 151,000 books on marriage, 27,000 books on dating, 12,000 books on attraction, and over 190,000 books on sex. Do any of these numbers surprise you? Why are there so many?

_____

_____

_____

It's so important for us to note that God physically created the man and woman. It is his idea, his plan. There is no point in the narrative where the Devil slips in and jacks stuff up.

How *does* Genesis 1:1 give us a starting point and hope for this conversation about marriage?

_____

_____

_____

What are a couple of differences between *dod* (which means "a mingling of souls") and the sex that we see in mass media today? What about the difference between biblical *dod* and how most church leaders talk about sex?

_____

_____

_____

Sex is God's idea.

MEN: Are there any truths in this message or the biblical passages that are tougher for you to live into? Some you might not want to really hear?

_____

_____

_____

What happens when sin is introduced into the cosmos is that it fractures everything.

LADIES: Are there any truths in this message or the biblical passages that are tougher for you to live into? Some you might not want to really hear?

_____

_____

_____

The story of the Bible is the story of God redeeming and reconciling to himself all that went wrong in the fall.

Summarize the teaching of this passage and this sermon in one sentence.

_____

_____

_____

A mingling of souls is far more sexy than anything you'll ever see on television or on the Internet.

Ten times out of ten, what we want (in sex) is not just the physical act but rather to be physically and intimately and deeply together with one another.

A mingling of souls is a type of sustaining force that mere physical sex just simply can't compete with.

The Song of Solomon will reveal to us the wise way and the foolish way to approach the opposite sex.

MEMORY VERSE

GENESIS 2:18

Then the LORD God said, "It is not good that the man should be alone; I will make him a helper fit for him."

DIVING DEEPER:
ONE APPLICATION

There are three factors working against this passage having any life change in you and me:

1] The fall has messed us all up. I don't care how brilliant, nice, and good-looking you are. You are messed up. And left to yourself, your heart will turn from God and to yourself.

2] This topic tends to carry baggage for many of us, as well as pre-conceived opinions. You might be doing something right now that the Bible calls foolish, and the temptation to fight will rear up in you.

3] A lot of what you are going to hear may run counter to what the world has told you and will tell you. It would be easier to side with what seems to be the majority opinion.

Please consider that this text is from the wisest man ever (Solomon) for the glory of God and the good of your soul.

Pray right now that God would keep your heart soft and open to the truth you hear. (If you are in a group setting, take some time to pray for those around you for the same thing.)

NOTES

TWO

THE LIST

I have met a bunch of (sorry for overgeneralization, but ...) girls in college and young adult women who have made a "list." You know the one. On this list is everything that a man must be in order for him to win her heart. If he is going to get the attention and affection of this young maiden for any extended period of time, he has to be of the highest caliber in so many ways. The overdetailed list usually has things such as: tall, dark, handsome, has whole Bible passages memorized in the original languages, hysterically funny but also serious, both strong but also sensitive, smart but does not know it, confident yet not arrogant, for sure wants kids but not too soon, has a certain hair color, all his teeth intact, nice legs, full-time doctor or lawyer with passion for Christ and missions, and owns a private beach where he rehabilitates orphaned seeing-eye dogs.

As women get older and their expectations of finding Mr. Right are hopelessly dashed, the list can tend to be narrowed down to two things: 1) Is he a dude? 2) Has he been to church before?

If so, "I do!"

Men are worse, though. This incredibly life-altering notion of what should our eventual spouse be like? ...

... they haven't given it much thought.

Men don't really take the time to make a list. We tend to take an "I'll know what I'm looking for when I see her" type of approach. (Which is really a lazy way of living into the fact that we don't like to sit around with the guys and make lists together in our pajamas.)

Between men and women, who is right and who is wrong? Probably both are both, to some degree. Whether you are male or female, whether or not you are a list person or an incredibly detailed planner type, there are at least a few things that should be on the list and some that should be off.

Bare minimums.
"If he isn't like *this*, I won't get near him."
"If she doesn't have *this* trait, I will run for the hills."

But where to begin? What should be at the forefront of our minds as we encounter the opposite sex?

SCRIPTURE

Here are some thoughts from wise Solomon.

SONG OF SOLOMON 1:1-6

[1:1]*The Song of Songs, which is Solomon's.*
The Bride Confesses Her Love

She

[2]*Let him kiss me with the kisses of his mouth!*
  For your love is better than wine;

[3]*your anointing oils are fragrant;*
  your name is oil poured out;
  therefore virgins love you.

[4]*Draw me after you; let us run.*
  The king has brought me into his chambers.

Others

  We will exult and rejoice in you;
  we will extol your love more than wine;
  rightly do they love you.

She

[5]*I am very dark, but lovely,*
  O daughters of Jerusalem,
  like the tents of Kedar,
  like the curtains of Solomon.

[6]*Do not gaze at me because I am dark,*
  because the sun has looked upon me.
  My mother's sons were angry with me;
  they made me keeper of the vineyards,
  but my own vineyard I have not kept!

DISCUSSION
QUESTIONS

You have never looked across the room and noticed someone's character.

Respond to this quote: "You have never looked across the room and noticed someone's character." If it's true, is that frustrating? Or is that just the way it is? No big deal?

_____

_____

_____

Solomon is apparently man-candy.

What is the significance of the book of Song of Solomon starting with: "Let him kiss me with the kisses of his mouth?" instead of "Wow, look how he serves at his church," or "He sure does know the Word," or "My, he tithes well." (Or some other character-based observation.)

_____

_____

_____

Matt gives two reasons why only being physically attracted to someone else can be dangerous. What were they? Are there more reasons that you can think of why having a relationship built only on physical attraction will eventually decline?

_____

_____

_____

In 1997, even Barbie had plastic surgery, literally.

Because of time, Matt did not get into "authority" in great detail, but of the few specific character traits to look for, he mentioned one in particular. Why would that be? What is it about "respect for authority" in particular that makes it important for people to have in their character? Are there other "top-tier" descriptors and character traits that need to be there?

_____

_____

_____

It is the Creator God of the universe who says we are fearfully and wonderfully made, not magazines and commercials.

Is it easier or harder for either gender to truly embrace who God made them in their gender? Said differently: "Is it harder for women to fully embrace their femininity, or for men to fully embrace their masculinity?"

_____

_____

_____

Your reputation is worth more than monetary wealth.

Summarize the teaching of this passage and this sermon in one sentence.

_____

_____

_____

There's a deep need in the human soul for companionship. It's not good for man to be alone.

The Bible is filled with examples of God engaging and redeeming in spite of relational carnage.

MEMORY VERSE

SONG OF SOLOMON 1:2

Let him kiss me with the kisses of his mouth!
For your love is better than wine.

DIVING DEEPER:
ONE APPLICATION

The world is pounding us with messages that physical attraction is all that matters. How can you have a renewed heart and mind this week so that it falls into its proper place in relationships? [Not ultimate, but not evil.] What is one way to apply this teaching to have a renewed mind in this area?

NOTES

THREE

HEAD KNOWLEDGE

There are so many things that we know are bad for us yet we do them anyway. "I know it's bad. I am going to do it anyway."

- We hate when everyone texts and drives because we know how dangerous it is, but we can handle it. We are very important and need to be sure to update our Facebook constantly ("turning right on Lancaster Avenue, feeling turny").
- I think that they have just stopped doing research on how bad smoking cigarettes is for you because everyone knows. Yet millions of people still rationalize smoking unapologetically.
- We can be reading a story about how someone died crazy-young of a heart-related problem, pause to pray for their family, and then continue eating our bacon guacamole burger made with extra gluten and a scoop of butter.

On a real basic level, we know in our hearts what is good or right and what is wrong or bad. That message oftentimes never gets down to our hands and feet when it comes time to act upon our beliefs.

Similarly, we *know* some things about dating. We *know* some obvious truths about how we should interact with the opposite sex. We *know* some dos and don'ts. The problem is that we know them in kind of a seminar format, meaning we could put together a great, organized presentation for *others* to hear about why *they* should make good choices in our relationships with the opposite sex.

The problem is that most of us need to sit in those lectures instead of give them.

We know what needs to be done, yet our flesh likes to take over and more often than not, we let it. In fact, I have lived in my flesh so many times and know too well the bent of my own heart that I am more convinced than anyone that any time I do right, it is by the grace of God alone.

I wonder what would happen if we actually heeded the warning signs around us and made our hands and feet do what our minds know? Imagine the difference in our lives and the lives around us! This is especially important when we talk about the most intimate of relationships we have. We must make good choices and it is so tough to do in these relationships.

First, let's make sure we see the God-ordained pattern to follow.

SCRIPTURE

SONG OF SOLOMON 1:7–2:7

^{1:7}Tell me, you whom my soul loves, where you pasture your flock, where you make it lie down at noon; for why should I be like one who veils herself beside the flocks of your companions?

Solomon and His Bride Delight in Each Other

He

⁸If you do not know, O most beautiful among women, follow in the tracks of the flock, and pasture your young goats beside the shepherds' tents. ⁹I compare you, my love, to a mare among Pharaoh's chariots. ¹⁰Your cheeks are lovely with ornaments, your neck with strings of jewels.

Others

¹¹We will make for you ornaments of gold, studded with silver.

She

¹²While the king was on his couch, my nard gave forth its fragrance. ¹³My beloved is to me a sachet of myrrh that lies between my breasts. ¹⁴My beloved is to me a cluster of henna blossoms in the vineyards of Engedi.

He

¹⁵Behold, you are beautiful, my love; behold, you are beautiful; your eyes are doves.

She

¹⁶Behold, you are beautiful, my beloved, truly delightful. Our couch is green; ¹⁷the beams of our house are cedar; our rafters are pine. ^{2:1}I am a rose of Sharon, a lily of the valleys.

He

²As a lily among brambles, so is my love among the young women.

She

³As an apple tree among the trees of the forest, so is my beloved among the young men. With great delight I sat in his shadow, and his fruit was sweet to my taste. ⁴He brought me to the banqueting house, and his banner over me was love.

SCRIPTURE

⁵*Sustain me with raisins; refresh me with apples, for I am sick with love.* ⁶*His left hand is under my head, and his right hand embraces me!* ⁷*I adjure you, O daughters of Jerusalem, by the gazelles or the does of the field, that you not stir up or awaken love until it pleases.*

NOTES

DISCUSSION
QUESTIONS

Let me just be straight, dating in our day and age is goofy.

Even if you love or hate the following categories of dating, give some pros and cons
(if possible) of each:
- traditional dating
- speed dating
- online dating
- the hookup culture

_____
_____
_____

If sex is what God says it is, there are few things as damaging to the human soul as the hookup culture.

Of course manipulation does not have positive long-term effects. But we probably have all
felt that pull on our soul to manipulate at times. Why is that? How can we avoid giving into
that?

_____
_____
_____

It sounds real nice to say, "If you are in a bad relationship, just get out." But what are ways
to do that that are God-honoring and get the job done?

_____
_____
_____

No amount of manipulation is going to be right and good in the long run.

> **If the relationship is exhausting, life-sucking, lacks clarity, or someone is playing games ... hit "eject."**

What are some ways that you can get hints of "showing initiative" from the other person? Does this still happen (or need to happen) in a marriage? How?

_____

_____

_____

> **Nothing ever good and godly happens between non-married dating couples when they lay on a couch, post ten o'clock to watch a movie.**

Fill in the blanks and discuss:

Sex within the confines of marriage is _____ .

Sex outside of the covenant of marriage is _____ .

> **It is not God's desire to keep from you any pleasure, but rather to lead you into the fullest pleasure possible.**

Summarize the teaching of this passage and this sermon in one sentence.

_____

_____

_____

> **It is not a bad or wrong thing to have a growing desire for sexual touch. It's not bad; it's God-designed.**

> **If you enter into the physical too quickly, you squelch and wound the ability to grow in actual intimacy with another person.**

MEMORY VERSE

PROVERBS 12:15

The way of a fool is right in his own eyes, but a wise man listens to advice.

DIVING DEEPER:
ONE APPLICATION

When we get in relationships, we tend to make our worst decisions based on emotions and not logic. It is vital to have someone who loves God and loves us, but who is slightly outside the relationship, giving us counsel. Who is the first person that you would go to with relationship questions, and if he or she told you any counsel, would you follow it? Name that person and this week let them know that they are that person for you.

NOTES

FOUR
DIPPING OUR TOES

My kids love going to the pool. You know how you can tell that I love it as well? Because I am willing to go through the lengthy "pool-excursion-prep" phase to get there. We have to go get suits on, get towels, get goggles, all sorts of floaties, kickboards, and swim toys. Then the sunscreen comes out and I have to get the kids to sit still while I apply it on them, which usually means that they will have a white handprint of their daddy on the middle of their back for a few days after. There's also the loading of bags with changes of clothes, pool shoes, regular shoes, and cover-ups.

The reason I go through all this is that I love being in the pool with my family, especially during the brutal Texas summers.

Getting in the pool is always fun, and my family does it all different ways. Most of us just jump right in, avoiding the slow cold that creeps up your body when you do the "walk-down-the-steps" entrance.

A couple of them, though, like to do the slow walk. They take their time. They move in tiny increments and wait ten minutes between each step for that half-inch of skin to get used to the temperature, and then move down another fraction of an inch. It seems like torture, but I see why they do it.

Just jumping right in can be scary.

In dating we see similar types of people. We see some that jump right in, perhaps way too quickly without even checking the temperature of the water. And others that take a painfully long time—too long— to get to where they will eventually be.

How can we strike that balance? How can we know how fast is moving too fast and how slow is too slow? We can gain some balance if we inform ourselves about a way to progress in relationships that has unfortunately almost disappeared in our culture.

We need to understand courtship.

SCRIPTURE

SONG OF SOLOMON 2:8–3:5

The Bride Adores Her Beloved

[8]The voice of my beloved! Behold, he comes, leaping over the mountains, bounding over the hills. [9]My beloved is like a gazelle or a young stag. Behold, there he stands behind our wall, gazing through the windows, looking through the lattice. [10]My beloved speaks and says to me: "Arise, my love, my beautiful one, and come away, [11]for behold, the winter is past; the rain is over and gone. [12]The flowers appear on the earth, the time of singing has come, and the voice of the turtledove is heard in our land. [13]The fig tree ripens its figs, and the vines are in blossom; they give forth fragrance. Arise, my love, my beautiful one, and come away. [14]O my dove, in the clefts of the rock, in the crannies of the cliff, let me see your face, let me hear your voice, for your voice is sweet, and your face is lovely. [15]Catch the foxes for us, the little foxes that spoil the vineyards, for our vineyards are in blossom." [16]My beloved is mine, and I am his; he grazes among the lilies. [17]Until the day breathes and the shadows flee, turn, my beloved, be like a gazelle or a young stag on cleft mountains.

[3:1]On my bed by night I sought him whom my soul loves; I sought him, but found him not. [2]I will rise now and go about the city, in the streets and in the squares; I will seek him whom my soul loves. I sought him, but found him not. [3]The watchmen found me as they went about in the city. "Have you seen him whom my soul loves?" [4]Scarcely had I passed them when I found him whom my soul loves. I held him, and would not let him go until I had brought him into my mother's house, and into the chamber of her who conceived me. [5]I adjure you, O daughters of Jerusalem, by the gazelles or the does of the field, that you not stir up or awaken love until it pleases.

QUESTIONS

Courtship is the time when you begin to date one person exclusively, frequently, and with the purpose of determining if this is the person you want to spend the rest of your life with.

How can a couple know when they have moved from *dating* into *courtship*?

_____

_____

_____

Moving forward in courtship is dangerous, risky, and awesome. And it can go bad.

Putting categories on things such as "dating" and "courtship" can run the risk of taking something fun and making it horribly unromantic. How can we think in these categories (or similar ones) and still keep the relationship as a real source of pleasure?

_____

_____

_____

To save dirty little secrets until after you get married creates a feeling similar to betrayal that might haunt you moving forward.

As you move into courtship, you often want to know more about a person's past so you can know how it affects him or her today. What are some specific areas not mentioned here you can think of to discuss? What questions can you ask that would bear fruitful discussion?

_____

_____

_____

In courtship you start navigating the tender spots.

What would your response be to a young, unmarried couple that say, "We know we are going to get married, so we are not going to wait?" What counsel would you give them?

_____

_____

_____

If a man or woman will not deal gently with your spiritual, emotional and intellectual wounds, why would you ever enter covenant with him or her?

Is it accurate or totally naive to say, "We are sexually compatible because I am a man and she is a woman?"

_____

_____

_____

The temptation in this stage is _We're going to get married, so why should we wait?_

Summarize the teaching of this passage and this sermon in one sentence.

_____

_____

_____

MEMORY VERSE

PROVERBS 3:5

I adjure you, O daughters of Jerusalem, by the gazelles or the does of the field, that you not stir up or awaken love until it pleases.

DIVING DEEPER:
ONE APPLICATION

Take time to read and meditate on the two stories that were shared at the end of the teaching. Read them slowly and afterward pause to reflect:
- The woman caught in adultery: John 8:1-11
- The woman at the well: John 4:1-27

NOTES

FIVE

THE BIG DAY

I get to do a lot of wedding ceremonies and let me tell you: It. Is. Awesome.

I love it. It's one of my very favorite things to do. I meet with the couples ahead of time and try to be a very active part of the ceremony instead of a diva preacher that pops in to marry them because the state of Texas acknowledges that I technically can, and then pops out after I snag my honorarium.

On wedding days I typically meet about forty-two thousand people and I love watching them try to figure out how to address me. Everyone wants to be respectful, but they are not sure how, depending on their background. I get stammering; a church-handshake and "Pastor," "Preacher," "Reverend," and "Pope Chandler;" and other odd things. I usually say, "I'm Matt" and just smile and get their names, letting them know it's good to meet them, because it genuinely is.

I get introduced to everyone in the room and get to go through this song and dance a lot, and now it is just fun for me. I meet a million people on those days, and generally do not remember many of them. Let's be honest, I just met forty-two thousand people in a ten-minute span and they all look alike in their suits and dresses. It's tough remembering all those names.

There are always two people that I never forget, though: The bride and the groom. I know their names. I know their hearts. I know their stories. Those are the two that are front and center on these days and their covenant before God is what matters on this day, so you better believe that we are on a first-name basis.

And then—get this—I get to stand before God as a witness and pronounce them married and say her new name for the first time. I get to say things like, "As a minister of the gospel of Jesus Christ, it is a privilege to pronounce you husband and wife, and I present to you this new family." What an honor. I have never had to look at any notes to remember what their names are. I know these two. This is a huge day where God is going to do something supernatural. This is a day that they will never forget and one I am so pumped to be a part of.

Everyone loves weddings, even dudes. It's time to look at Solomon's big day. You think you have seen cool weddings? Wait until you see this ...

SCRIPTURE

SONG OF SOLOMON 3:6–11

Solomon Arrives for the Wedding

⁶What is that coming up from the wilderness like columns of smoke, perfumed with myrrh and frankincense, with all the fragrant powders of a merchant? ⁷Behold, it is the litter of Solomon! Around it are sixty mighty men, some of the mighty men of Israel, ⁸all of them wearing swords and expert in war, each with his sword at his thigh, against terror by night. ⁹King Solomon made himself a carriage from the wood of Lebanon. ¹⁰He made its posts of silver, its back of gold, its seat of purple; its interior was inlaid with love by the daughters of Jerusalem. ¹¹Go out, O daughters of Zion, and look upon King Solomon, with the crown with which his mother crowned him on the day of his wedding, on the day of the gladness of his heart.

DISCUSSION
QUESTIONS

At a wedding, it's all beautiful and feels right, but there's something going on underneath it, and if we don't get to what's roaring underneath it, then we're kind of going to miss the point.

If you are married, what was a highlight of your wedding day? If you are not married, what would you anticipate a highlight being? After hearing this teaching on the sacredness and meaning of a wedding, is there anything you would plan to do differently?

_____

_____

_____

One of the profound moments in a wedding ceremony is the entrance of the bride, who is adorned in white garments. What's going on in that moment, according to the Word of God, is a shadow of the reality of how God looks upon his Church.

Matt talks about the fact that "you-time" after you get married is pretty much nonexistent. What are practical ways you can try to work some into your schedule so you can have that time?

_____

_____

_____

God has not just called us to love one another but to love with a very particular type of love.

In the Bible, repeatedly, the root sin that plagues men is passivity.

> **My role as the father of two daughters is to get them to a point where they don't need me and to hand them off to a man for the last half of their life who will show them the care, love, and nurture I've had the privilege of showing them from the second they breathed their first breath right up until I walk them down that aisle.**

Fill in the blank with the first word(s) that come to mind "Passive men _____"

How can a man strike the balance of being an initiator, but not overbearing?

_____

_____

_____

> **The weight of pursuit, the heft of initiation—almost all of that falls on the shoulders of the man.**

What kinds of things can women do to help men avoid passivity?

_____

_____

_____

The root sin that plagues men is passivity. What might the root sin for women be?

_____

_____

_____

Summarize the teaching of this passage and this sermon in one sentence.

_____

_____

_____

MEMORY VERSE

EPHESIANS 5:28

In the same way husbands should love their wives as their own bodies. He who loves his wife loves himself.

DIVING DEEPER:
ONE APPLICATION

There was mention that there is not "the one" for you. For most of us, that is a change in thinking about the one we are with (or looking for). What are the implications of that (very unsentimental) truth?

NOTES

SIX

THE BIG NIGHT

Ladies, you know how you have been planning your wedding day since you were a fetus? He has been thinking of the wedding night since puberty.

This is the big night. It is the first night when two people give themselves to each other under the covenant of marriage. And it is bigger than a *big deal*.

Sex has the power to completely alter a relationship. A great sex life, based on true intimacy, can help a man and woman feel the ultimate connectedness. It can make them think even if the whole world is against them, they are for each other. In their moments of feeling alone, sex can help a couple remember that God gave someone to them.

Our culture has a completely messed-up view on the topic and feeds us lies by the boatload:

- Women have male sex drives.
- Inconsequential sex with strangers leaves no hole in your soul.
- One-night stands are the normal way to live a healthy life.
- Your manhood is tied to the number of girls your sleep with.

All garbage. It's time to replace that trash with truth.

Although some of you might get squeamish, it is time to look at this topic that so greatly impacts us, that our culture has lied to us about, and about which the church has historically shut its mouth.

In the Song of Solomon, we not only get a model of godly sexuality on a wedding night, but it is far from a thirty-thousand-foot view. Of all the things that God has chosen to preserve for us for a few thousand years, he chose this most intimate of moments between a husband and wife.

There must be a reason.

SCRIPTURE

SONG OF SOLOMON 4:1–15

Solomon Admires His Bride's Beauty

[4:1]Behold, you are beautiful, my love, behold, you are beautiful! Your eyes are doves behind your veil. Your hair is like a flock of goats leaping down the slopes of Gilead. [2]Your teeth are like a flock of shorn ewes that have come up from the washing, all of which bear twins, and not one among them has lost its young. [3]Your lips are like a scarlet thread, and your mouth is lovely. Your cheeks are like halves of a pomegranate behind your veil. [4]Your neck is like the tower of David, built in rows of stone; on it hang a thousand shields, all of them shields of warriors. [5]Your two breasts are like two fawns, twins of a gazelle, that graze among the lilies. [6]Until the day breathes and the shadows flee, I will go away to the mountain of myrrh and the hill of frankincense. [7]You are altogether beautiful, my love; there is no flaw in you. [8]Come with me from Lebanon, my bride; come with me from Lebanon. Depart from the peak of Amana, from the peak of Senir and Hermon, from the dens of lions, from the mountains of leopards. [9]You have captivated my heart, my sister, my bride; you have captivated my heart with one glance of your eyes, with one jewel of your necklace. [10]How beautiful is your love, my sister, my bride! How much better is your love than wine, and the fragrance of your oils than any spice! [11]Your lips drip nectar, my bride; honey and milk are under your tongue; the fragrance of your garments is like the fragrance of Lebanon. [12]A garden locked is my sister, my bride, a spring locked, a fountain sealed. [13]Your shoots are an orchard of pomegranates with all choicest fruits, henna with nard, [14]nard and saffron, calamus and cinnamon, with all trees of frankincense, myrrh and aloes, with all choice spices— [15]a garden fountain, a well of living water, and flowing streams from Lebanon.

Let's understand real intimacy before we begin to introduce the physical aspect that will take our intimacy to another level. Let's lay the foundation before we build the house.

In this text he affirms his bride by telling her things like, "Your teeth are all there!" and "When I look at your hair, I think of goats!" That would not fly today and would probably ruin the mood. What are some ways in our culture that a man can offer nongeneric, heartfelt compliments to his bride?

_____

_____

_____

The desire is not just for a physical act but the consummation of an intimacy that has been hard-fought and protected until God has let it off the leash.

Fill in this blank: "God in his goodness has given us the gift of sex. The world has taken that gift and _____ ."

One of the things that becomes imperative to notice about Solomon's love for this woman is that his love for her, although he delights in her physically, is not a physical love alone but rather is built upon the foundation that was laid before it got physical.

All of this (how Solomon approached his wife tenderly and slowly) speaks to the value and the dignity that he sees in and speaks into the soul of his wife.

> **"Yes, yes, yes. I love this, but I love *you*. I want *you*. I love *you*." He's just not going to get off of that track.**

Where do most people you know get their perceptions of what sex should be? Where did/do you get yours?

_____

_____

_____

What are some reasons to have some other people in your life with whom you can talk about intimate details of your sex life? Why not just keep it between you and your spouse?

_____

_____

_____

> **One of the reasons I want to just plead with young men in particular about the dangers of pornography is because if you come into your wedding night with images like that in your head, you will not treat your bride as of utmost value, with intrinsic worth and dignity and with depth of soul.**

Contrast the sex that Solomon and his bride experienced to the sex we see in the movies and television today. What is different?

_____

_____

_____

What is the significance of marriage being a covenant and not a contract?

_____

_____

_____

Summarize the teaching of this passage and this sermon in one sentence.

_____

_____

_____

> **I'm wired in a lot of ways that are completely unacceptable for me to just sit in.**

MEMORY VERSE

SONG OF SOLOMON 4:7

You are altogether beautiful, my love; there is no flaw in you.

DIVING DEEPER:
ONE APPLICATION

Write this somewhere you will see it (a mirror, wallet, purse, cell phone wallpaper, etc.) several times until we meet again as a group, phrased appropriately for your life stage: "I entered into a covenant, not a contract."

NOTES

SEVEN

NOT US!

Before I got married I asked a million questions.
I wanted to know about money.
I wanted to know about sex.
I wanted to know about communication.
I wanted to know about sex again.

I never knew that I needed to ask about conflict. Why would I? I looked at all the old married people who fought and thought, *Good thing that will never be us. We agree on everything! If we didn't agree on everything, why would we get married?*

Now I do premarital counseling and I talk with them about conflict. The ones who worry me the least are ones who can tell me stories of deep hurt that has been dealt with and re-solved. The ones who worry me the most are the moon-eyed doofuses that naively giggle to each other about how they don't ever fight about anything.

Me: So what are you going to do when you disagree?
Them: I guess we just never will.
Me: What if you disappoint the other one?
Them: Impossible!
Me: If you were ever to get mad at each other...
Them: [cutting me off] Not us!
[I pause, drink my coffee, and think of mean things to say.]

Conflict is a part of life, and especially marriage. The great goal is not to avoid all conflict, but to love each other and honor Christ in it.

Be ready for it; it is coming. Here's what to do.

SCRIPTURE

SONG OF SOLOMON 5:2–5

The Bride Searched for Her Beloved

[5:2] I slept, but my heart was awake. A sound! My beloved is knocking. "Open to me, my sister, my love, my dove, my perfect one, for my head is wet with dew, my locks with the drops of the night." [3] I had put off my garment; how could I put it on? I had bathed my feet; how could I soil them? [4] My beloved put his hand to the latch, and my heart was thrilled within me. [5] I arose to open to my beloved, and my hands dripped with myrrh, my fingers with liquid myrrh, on the handles of the bolt.

DISCUSSION
QUESTIONS

20 percent of the Song of Solomon is on conflict.

Does the fact that so much of this book is about conflict encourage you or discourage you, and why?

_____

_____

_____

Conflict is a part of the healthiest, most romantic, most passionate relationships.

"All frustrations in life result from unmet expectations." What are some expectations that you have for your significant other that sometimes cause conflict? Does he or she know them? Are they hard to articulate?

_____

_____

_____

Sex is messy. The only place it's not messy is on television.

The time when the husband gets home from work and has expectations on the wife (food ready, kids civilized, etc.) can cause a lot of conflict in marriage. How can a couple not have this conflict? What are some practical ways to not have this be a point of stress?

_____

_____

_____

All frustrations in life result from unmet expectations.

In the end, it is a risky thing to pursue your spouse sexually.

You cannot control your spouse, but you can control yourself. Yet we so often try to change our spouses and not ourselves. Talk about this temptation to try to change your spouse and ignore changing yourself first.

_____

_____

_____

In the heat of the moment, sometimes it is good to just walk away. How hard is that for you? When you've done that, does it usually help or do you just come back and have a case built as to why you are even more right?

_____

_____

_____

Covenant isn't "I'm going to give to get" but "I'm going to give to give."

Talk about the difference between *reacting* and *responding*. Would changing the terminology help you in your relationship?

_____

_____

_____

Summarize the teaching of this passage and this sermon in one sentence.

_____

_____

_____

MEMORY VERSE

SONG OF SOLOMON 5:4

My beloved put his hand to the latch, and my heart was thrilled within me.

DIVING DEEPER:
ONE APPLICATION

Try losing every single argument this week with your spouse. (Yes, I'm dead serious.) Admit your fault in the situation and ignore your spouse. What is the effect on your relationship?

NOTES

EIGHT

OWN IT

Me: Go apologize to your brother.
Kid #1: I'm sorry that you got hurt when my fist hit you.
Me: That is not really an apology, sweetie.
Kid #1: I'm sorry but you made me super mad so I hit you and now you are crying like the baby that you are.
Me: Try again, sweetheart.
Kid #1: (exasperated – decides to talk like a politician) Mistakes were made...
Me: Nope.
Kid #1 (shrugs shoulders)
Me: (exasperated) Say you're sorry and I'll give you candy.
Kid #1: (lighting up) I'm soooooooo sorry! Give me candy, Daddy!
Kid #1 (runs off happily eating candy. Dad is proud, assuming she has learned her lesson.)
Kid #2: (punches kid #3) Sorry. (Holds out his hand for candy.)

Okay, that has never really happened, but you can see it playing out, right? One kid offended another and the other one punched him. Then it's apology time, but what happens? They both see the fault in the other and are blind to their own tiny little transgression.

The sad thing is that we all often are like children and do what I call "fake apologies." We hate taking responsibility for our mistakes, and most of us have not learned the art of apologizing well. The bummer is that this is one skill that can totally revolutionize relationships. Think about it: The person who is quick to apologize well and never holds a grudge always has people who want to be around him. The lady who admits her faults without feeling the need to point out the fault in others is highly esteemed and thought of tenderly.

Our media, as usual, is no help at teaching us this skill. In fact, TV shows tend to go to one of two extremes. Either: "You have wronged me so much, I will never forgive you." Or, the other extreme: laughing off offenses that would hurt deeply in real life.

We don't learn from anyplace how to apologize well.

Luckily, Solomon and his girl have something to say about it.

SCRIPTURE

SONG OF SOLOMON 5:6—6:10

5:6I opened to my beloved, but my beloved had turned and gone. My soul failed me when he spoke. I sought him, but found him not; I called him, but he gave no answer. 7The watchmen found me as they went about in the city; they beat me, they bruised me, they took away my veil, those watchmen of the walls. 8I adjure you, O daughters of Jerusalem, if you find my beloved, that you tell him I am sick with love.

Others

9What is your beloved more than another beloved, O most beautiful among women? What is your beloved more than another beloved, that you thus adjure us?

The Bride Praises Her Beloved

She

10My beloved is radiant and ruddy, distinguished among ten thousand. 11His head is the finest gold; his locks are wavy, black as a raven. 12His eyes are like doves beside streams of water, bathed in milk, sitting beside a full pool. 13His cheeks are like beds of spices, mounds of sweet-smelling herbs. His lips are lilies, dripping liquid myrrh. 14His arms are rods of gold, set with jewels. His body is polished ivory, bedecked with sapphires. 15His legs are alabaster columns, set on bases of gold. His appearance is like Lebanon, choice as the cedars. 16His mouth is most sweet, and he is altogether desirable. This is my beloved and this is my friend, O daughters of Jerusalem.

Others

6:1Where has your beloved gone, O most beautiful among women? Where has your beloved turned, that we may seek him with you?

Together in the Garden of Love

She

2My beloved has gone down to his garden to the beds of spices, to graze in the gardens and to gather lilies. 3I am my beloved's and my beloved is mine; he grazes among the lilies.

SCRIPTURE

Solomon and His Bride Delight in Each Other

He

⁴You are beautiful as Tirzah, my love, lovely as Jerusalem, awesome as an army with banners. ⁵Turn away your eyes from me, for they overwhelm me—Your hair is like a flock of goats leaping down the slopes of Gilead. ⁶Your teeth are like a flock of ewes that have come up from the washing; all of them bear twins; not one among them has lost its young. ⁷Your cheeks are like halves of a pomegranate behind your veil. ⁸There are sixty queens and eighty concubines, and virgins without number. ⁹My dove, my perfect one, is the only one, the only one of her mother, pure to her who bore her. The young women saw her and called her blessed; the queens and concubines also, and they praised her. ¹⁰"Who is this who looks down like the dawn, beautiful as the moon, bright as the sun, awesome as an army with banners?"

NOTES

It's a painful thing to have things about y... revealed that you don't want revealed about you, is it not?

What exactly makes it so difficult to initiate owning our responsibility in a conflict? Why are sincere, or "actual," apologies so difficult?

_____

_____

_____

I have never been a part of a fight or come across a fight that has been 100 percent one person's fault.

"I apologize if you were offended." "I'm sorry I did X, but you did Y." What are some other examples of *fake apologies*?

_____

_____

_____

We initiate and own (our mistakes) because if we will not, then we give the Devil a foothold in our relationships.

Discuss a better solution than this: When I run to my friend in a conflict, I generally tell only my side of the story where I am most right and my spouse's side of the story where my spouse is most wrong. My friend affirms me and bashes my spouse, making that time thoroughly unhelpful and possibly even harmful.

_____

_____

_____

> a woman connects with her girls or a guy con-
> ..s with his guys, what can commonly take place in
> .e fight is, "Tell me about my strengths; compare my
> trengths to her weaknesses so I can feel right and
> good about where I am in the fight."

Over time in a relationship, we can start to take our significant other's strengths (the reason we married them in the first place) for granted and blow all their weaknesses out of proportion. Why does that happen and how can we avoid it? What would a marriage look like that does the opposite?

_____

_____

_____

A quote from the teaching is: "When a person is repentant for their sin, when they're owning their part, that is not the time to correct further and to rehash yet again just to make sure they get it." Based on that, fill in this blank: "When a person is repentant for their sin, when they're owning their part, the wisest next step that you can take as the offended party is to

_____ ."

> She will not give in to the urge of listing out his
> weaknesses in comparison with her strengths.

Do you have any examples in your life of times you have been extended grace and therefore were able to more easily extend it to another?

_____

_____

_____

> When a person is repentant for their sin, when
> they're owning their part, that is not the time to
> correct further and to rehash yet again just to make
> sure they get it.

Summarize the teaching of this passage and this sermon in one sentence.

_____

_____

_____

> Where we have experienced grace, our ability to
> extend it exponentially increases.

MEMORY VERSE

EPHESIANS 4:26–27

Be angry and do not sin; do not let the sun go down on your anger, and give no opportunity to the devil.

DIVING DEEPER:
ONE APPLICATION

Apply what was mentioned specifically in the message: "Pull out a piece of paper and begin to list all that is good and right in your spouse. All that you love about them. All that you are grateful to God that they do for you."

NOTES

NINE

BATTLE-CHOOSING

As a parent, I have to let some things go.

I cannot possibly correct every error I see in my kids or I wouldn't be able to leave for work. Ever. There are some things that are worth fighting, and some things worth just letting go.

You've heard "choose your battles." Never is that more true than in parenting.

Battle not worth the fight: My son yelling outside a little louder than I'd like him to, probably being heard by the neighbors.

Good battle to fight: My son raising his voice to my bride.

Bad battle to fight: Kids fighting over the monkey bars, and they eventually work it out.

Good battle to fight: Kids punching each other in the face.

Battle not worth the fight: My son not being able to spell a word he'll never use again on his 2nd grade spelling test when he's doing his homework at 11PM.

Good battle to fight: My daughter dangling her brother off the balcony by his ankles.

You get the idea.

There are some battles just worth avoiding altogether. Some are not worth our time so we can keep our sanity.

There is one battle that almost all married couples do not even begin. And they must. Actually, most of us forget it is even a battle to be fought or not. One of Satan's most clever lies was to trick us into thinking that this is not a battle worth fighting.

It is.

SCRIPTURE

SONG OF SOLOMON 7:1–11

7:1How beautiful are your feet in sandals, O noble daughter! Your rounded thighs are like jewels, the work of a master hand. 2Your navel is a rounded bowl that never lacks mixed wine. Your belly is a heap of wheat, encircled with lilies. 3Your two breasts are like two fawns, twins of a gazelle. 4Your neck is like an ivory tower. Your eyes are pools in Heshbon, by the gate of Bath-rabbim. Your nose is like a tower of Lebanon, which looks toward Damascus. 5Your head crowns you like Carmel, and your flowing locks are like purple; a king is held captive in the tresses. 6How beautiful and pleasant you are, O loved one, with all your delights! 7Your stature is like a palm tree, and your breasts are like its clusters. 8I say I will climb the palm tree and lay hold of its fruit. Oh may your breasts be like clusters of the vine, and the scent of your breath like apples, 9and your mouth like the best wine.

She

It goes down smoothly for my beloved, gliding over lips and teeth. 10I am my beloved's, and his desire is for me.

The Bride Gives Her Love

11Come, my beloved, let us go out into the fields and lodge in the villages;

> Our love isn't, "Make me feel this way if you want me to stay." That's not how we love. Our love is, "I'm giving myself to you regardless."

There were a series of questions I asked at the end of the teaching to discuss further.

What are the strengths in your wife (husband)?

_____

_____

_____

> Christians cannot fall out of love because our love is not predicated upon emotions alone but rather finds its strength in the covenant.

What do you need to own? Where might you seek forgiveness? Where have you lacked grace?

_____

_____

_____

> See, husbands and wives, one of the real gifts that God has given to you and me is the treasure hunt of finding these things in our spouses that no one else knows is there.

Where do you see your spouse excelling, and where do you spot strength and dignity in those things?

_____

_____

_____

> **Men, women, here's the first thing you have to do: pay attention. You have this opportunity to see things that no one else is going to get to see.**

How can you begin to just throw a little dry wood there on that fire and begin to breathe back into it? Where can we get fuel and begin to pour it on?

_____

_____

_____

> **Pay attention to the desires, the strengths, the growth of your spouse, the things that only you get to see. Mine for those. Look for those. Be dialed in. Pay attention.**

What are the barriers to playfulness, and how can you be more playful?

_____

_____

_____

> **Don't get so crusty. Be playful. But be playful in a way that your wife or husband enjoys, not in a way that gets on their nerves.**

Summarize the teaching of this passage and this sermon in one sentence.

_____

_____

_____

> **Fight for fun. Fight for it.**

MEMORY VERSE

How beautiful and pleasant you are, O loved one, with all your delights!

DIVING DEEPER:
ONE APPLICATION

This week, throw off all your inhibitions and do something completely unexpectedly playful with your spouse. That's your difficult homework: play. Play hard.

NOTES

TEN

LOVEY-DOVEY

Just to make me throw up in my mouth a little bit, I took a walk through the local greeting-card store and noted a few of the messages from cards in the romance section.

Here's a snapshot of actual cards for sale on the shelf:
  -*The joy to be found in winter's season is easily found with you.*
  -*The rose speaks of love silently, in a language known only to the heart.*
  -*If you're a bird, I'm a bird.* [Yes, this one really exists.]
  -*I don't know how I am still alive. I have given my beating heart to you.* [How sweet.]
  -*Love is not written on paper for it can be erased. Nor is it etched on stone, for stone can be broken. But it is inscribed on the heart where it can remain forever.*
  -*If I could have just one wish, I would wish to wake up every day to the sound of your breath on my neck, the warmth of your lips on my cheek, the touch of your fingers on my skin, and the feel of your heart beating with mine... knowing that I could never find that feeling with anyone other than you.* [That is actually four wishes but... whatever...]
  -*I carry your heart with me. I carry it in my heart.* [Not sure what this even means.]

When I see all this nonsense about hearts being in ours, love making the winter more chipper, and giving my woman my still-beating heart, it makes me a bit sick, and in my spirit I rebel against everything they represent. In fact, most people go one of two directions—love it or hate it. [It's no mystery which way I lean.]

But in leaning away from all this greeting-card garbage, some, like me, have maybe gone too far and we can tend to take all the romance completely out of our marriages. That, too, is so dangerous and downright unbiblical.

We do it great as dating couples and terrible as married couples? Why is that? How do we get it back?

SCRIPTURE

SONG OF SOLOMON 7:11–13

The Bride Gives Her Love

[11]Come, my beloved, let us go out into the fields and lodge in the villages; [12]let us go out early to the vineyards and see whether the vines have budded, whether the grape blossoms have opened and the pomegranates are in bloom. There I will give you my love. [13]The mandrakes give forth fragrance, and beside our doors are all choice fruits, new as well as old, which I have laid up for you, O my beloved.

QUESTIONS

Some people are really turned off by the idea that romance is to be disciplined. But it is! Especially as life gets moving, there must be discipline.

When you think of "romantic," what people and images immediately come to mind? Why did you pick those people and images in particular?

_____

_____

_____

Most men just throw all the weight of their romance on three national holidays.

What are small, practical ways that men can be more romantic with women?

_____

_____

_____

The brunt of romantic pursuit falls on the shoulders of the man.

What are small practical ways that women can be more romantic with men?

_____

_____

_____

Wives hold an unbelievable amount of power over the emotional and intellectual well-being of their husbands.

Get away. Break up the monotony.

What makes getaways difficult at your life stage?

_____

_____

_____

Probably the greatest enemy of keeping the fire burning is just laziness.

What kind of getaways are practical for you and your spouse? Actual vacations? Coffee in the morning? Date night every week?

_____

_____

_____

Summarize the teaching of this passage and this sermon in one sentence.

_____

_____

_____

MEMORY VERSE

SONG OF SOLOMON 7:11

Come, my beloved, let us go out into the fields and lodge in the villages.

DIVING DEEPER:
ONE APPLICATION

MEN: Talk to your spouse and ask, "How can I be more romantic with you?"

WOMEN: Remember that you hold a lot of power over your husbands. This week, let every single mistake he makes ... go. Forget about it. Just take a week to be positive and encouraging and see what happens.

NOTES

ELEVEN

THE STUPID TAX

I pastor a church with a lot of young people in it, and there is such an energy in our congregation. That bunch of young people who gather to praise Jesus are naive enough to believe the Bible when it says that the gospel can actually change the entire world.

So many pastors tell me that they wish they had a church like mine, with more young people, and lament that their congregations have just "gotten so old." (Ironically some of these young pastors, who think Jesus can do anything, don't think he can change the heart of some old church curmudgeons.)

But they hopefully really know this truth deep down: the older generation is vital.

In the young we have energy, but in the old we have life experience.
In the young we have wide-eyes, but in the old we have wise ones.

The old have made way more mistakes than hopefully the younger generation will ever make. They have paid what has been affectionately called "the stupid tax." They have messed up. Hard. And paid the price. Some of them lived through recession, horrible money choices, multiple terrible marriages, and more. They have seen more depravity than we have at our age and know so many pitfalls we can avoid. Why do we not parade those people up front every week and just let them talk? Think about how much we could learn from them! How much time could we young, dumb people save by just listening and applying their wisdom?

On the flip side, how much has the older generation done right? In business, in marriage, in spiritual disciplines, in friendships, with money, and more?

I love the times I get to sit down with old men. In those moments I do something that is quite rare for me.

I shut my mouth and listen.

The only time I open it is to ask them to "keep going." When they talk, I want to devour every word they say. I want to feast on all their wisdom.

In the passage today, we get a glimpse of Solomon and his bride in their old age. Eat. This. Up.

SCRIPTURE

SONG OF SOLOMON 8:1–7

Longing for Her Beloved

8:1Oh that you were like a brother to me who nursed at my mother's breasts! If I found you outside, I would kiss you, and none would despise me. 2I would lead you and bring you into the house of my mother—she who used to teach me. I would give you spiced wine to drink, the juice of my pomegranate. 3His left hand is under my head, and his right hand embraces me! 4I adjure you, O daughters of Jerusalem, that you not stir up or awaken love until it pleases. 5Who is that coming up from the wilderness, leaning on her beloved? Under the apple tree I awakened you. There your mother was in labor with you; there she who bore you was in labor. 6Set me as a seal upon your heart, as a seal upon your arm, for love is strong as death, jealousy is fierce as the grave. Its flashes are flashes of fire, the very flame of the Lord. 7Many waters cannot quench love, neither can floods drown it. If a man offered for love all the wealth of his house, he would be utterly despised.

DISCUSSION
QUESTIONS

One of the things that we see as an overriding idea in this very strange text is despite the fact that they've got all of this history, they're still pursuing one another.

Picture your life when you are *old*. What immediately comes to mind? What would bring you joy in your old age? What would bring you sorrow?

_____

_____

_____

If we will finish strong, we will fight the drift toward just being good roommates. Just sharing a checkbook and a bed. We will fight for further intimacy.

The two in this story "refuse to become just good roommates." Obviously no couples ever want to be just roommates, but it happens. How? How can it be avoided? Pretend you are giving advice to an unmarried couple about how to avoid this. What would you say?

_____

_____

_____

We have an insatiable desire for greater depth, greater love, greater understanding, greater insight, the ability to see more clearly the heart and mind of our spouses. This is what's going on. This is how longevity occurs.

Two different types of love are described in this session: *Ahava* (an unquenchable love based on a covenant promise) and *rayah* (sort of a "friendly" love). Flesh those out a bit as a group. When you picture a marriage filled with ahava, what images comes to mind? What about when you picture one with rayah?

_____

_____

_____

I think one of the bigger lies that befalls people is this grand expectation that they've found somebody that's going to complete them.

Do you get the sense that most people feel as though they are *owed* a marriage? An easy marriage? A certain *way* that a spouse is supposed to be? If so, where does that idea come from? What are some damaging implications of having those preconceived expectations?

_____

_____

_____

Be prepared for dark days, dark months, dark years. It's a broken world and nobody gets out without bleeding.

Summarize the teaching of this passage and this sermon in one sentence.

_____

_____

_____

As we get near the end of this study together (one more session), reflect as a group. Is there anything from a previous session that is worth talking about again?

_____

_____

_____

MEMORY VERSE

SONG OF SOLOMON 8:7

Many waters cannot quench love, neither can floods drown it.

DIVING DEEPER:
ONE APPLICATION

I shared in this session one way that I act that can hurt my wife deeply and can be a default way of acting if I feel like I am *losing*. I can use my words to cut. Deep. It is stupid and wrong, yet something that I know is there as a weapon if I need it. What is that *thing* for you? Is it a hot temper? Your tongue? Manipulation? Withholding sex? A sin in their past that you can bring up to shame them? Name it.

Declare that temptation for you and lay it specifically before Jesus.

NOTES

TWELVE

THE END

Well, this is it: the last session.

Here is my candid prayer for you: that the truth in this great book, the Song of Solomon, does not fall flat.
- That this study was more than just fun.
- That is was more than just a time of feeling guilty and then trying real hard to change.
- That it was more than just a few videos that had points where you could elbow your spouse to make sure he heard it.
- That this was more than just a time to get together, eat junk food, and check "small group" off your Christian to-do list.

My hope as we wrap up is that you would look back over this material and review it. What stuck out to you? What was so convicting at the moment but maybe has slipped your mind? Use your notes or this book to jog your memory. After tonight, put this on your shelf so you can refer back to it in the weeks, months, or years to come.

This sacred literature, through the power of the Spirit, has the power to change us. It really does.

That's why I love this Book and the One who inspired it.

And as a Christian, I can honestly say that I love and care about you and your relationships as well.

So I earnestly pray that this last teaching would be transformative, eye-opening, helpful, and Christ-honoring.

It's been a privilege.

Here we go—one last time.

SCRIPTURE

SONG OF SOLOMON 8:8–14

Final Advice
Others

⁸We have a little sister, and she has no breasts. What shall we do for our sister on the day when she is spoken for? ⁹If she is a wall, we will build on her a battlement of silver, but if she is a door, we will enclose her with boards of cedar.

She

¹⁰I was a wall, and my breasts were like towers; then I was in his eyes as one who finds peace. ¹¹Solomon had a vineyard at Baal-hamon; he let out the vineyard to keepers; each one was to bring for its fruit a thousand pieces of silver. ¹²My vineyard, my very own, is before me; you, O Solomon, may have the thousand, and the keepers of the fruit two hundred.

He

¹³O you who dwell in the gardens, with companions listening for your voice; let me hear it.

She

¹⁴Make haste, my beloved, and be like a gazelle or a young stag on the mountains of spices.

D I S C U S S I O N
QUESTIONS

There is no experience of joy or loss that has not been redeemed by Christ and now is used by and can be used by the Holy Spirit of God to minister to others.

This session talks about how we need to share our stories with younger folks. Starting those relationships ("Hey, can I mentor you?") is awkward and sounds really cocky. How can those relationships form? How can that actually happen so you can pass along your successes and failures?

_____

_____

_____

As the Lord grows you, heals you, and begins to create a new relational dynamic in your marriage, your experiences are invaluable.

Take this opportunity right now to sharpen each other: what are some things that you have learned in your relationship that you would pass along to the group? Is there one key truth or practice that has been particularly helpful for you?

_____

_____

_____

The cross would bid me share.

We tend to have individual ways we serve God, but what are ways you can serve the Lord together?

_____

_____

_____

One of the keys to longevity is serving the Lord together.

The book ends very similar to how it began: with pursuit, desire, and hope.

Respond to this statement so it won't just feel like just a good Christian bumper sticker: "To have a mingling of souls, you must have Jesus." What does that even mean?

_____

_____

_____

Your need for a Savior will never be more apparent to you than when you're trying to faithfully walk in the wisdom laid out in this book.

As we conclude this study together, reflect as a group. Is there anything from a previous session that is worth talking about again?

_____

_____

_____

Summarize the teaching of this passage and this sermon in one sentence.

_____

_____

_____

May we pursue one another often, for the glory of his name and to reflect all the more the beauty of his romantic pursuit of us as his covenant people.

MEMORY VERSE

SONG OF SOLOMON 8:14
Make haste, my beloved, and be like a gazelle or a young stag on the mountains of spices.

DIVING DEEPER:
ONE APPLICATION

1] Set aside about 20 minutes.
2] **MEN**, mediate on: Titus 2:2.
Older men are to be sober-minded; dignified; self-controlled; sound in faith, in love, and in steadfastness.

WOMEN, mediate on Titus 2:3-5.
Older women, likewise, are to be reverent in behavior, not slanderers or slaves to much wine. They are to teach what is good, and so train the young women to love their husbands and children, to be self-controlled, pure, working at home, kind, and submissive to their own husbands, that the word of God may not be reviled.

3] Write what God speaks to you in this time.

_____
_____
_____
_____
_____
_____

NOTES

BEHIND THE BOOK
MINGLING OF SOULS

SONG OF SOLOMON

INTRODUCTIONS

The twenty-second book in the Old Testament, the Song of Solomon, is often referred to as the "Song of Songs" as well, the name being a Hebrew superlative, the same way in which the Bible speaks of the King of Kings, Lord of Lords, or Holy of Holies. The title *the Song of Songs* is a Hebrew idiom meaning "The Most Excellent Song." This supreme song has been "breathed out by God" (2 Tim. 3:16) and preserved for centuries in our biblical canon by God's good grace with timeless truths for us all.

THE AUTHOR

Immediately in the title we see that the author of the Song of Solomon appears to be Solomon, but is it really that simple? There are numerous reasons to take the author as Solomon, or at the least someone transcribing the thoughts of the great king of Israel. Solomon, the son of David and third king of Israel, is named in the book as author, and his name appears seven times in the text (1:1, 5; 3:7, 9, 11; 8:11–12). There are characteristics of the book that make it very natural to assume that Solomon was the author as well. "The fact that Solomon was known for his wisdom and poetry (1 Kings 4:29–34) partially substantiates his authorship of this book." "The allusions to nature fit in with Solomon's interests (1 Kings 4:33). Also, references to royal horses …, and the palanquin tend to support Solomonic authorship. The geographical references suggest that the places were all in one united kingdom, which was true chiefly during Solomon's reign. Thus, there is every reason to accept the traditional view of authorship, and contrary arguments are not convincing."

The evidence points us to Solomon as author of this book, inspired by the Spirit of God like every other biblical author (2 Pet. 1:21). "King Solomon probably wrote this loveliest of his 1,005 songs (1 Kings 4:32) some time during his forty year reign (971–931 BC)." What we will soon see is that the book written by someone thousands of years ago and thousands of miles away is still incredibly relevant for us today.

INTERPRETIVE APPROACHES

How to properly read the Song of Songs has been debated by scholars and theologians for centuries. Over the years it has been interpreted several different ways, though the different interpretations can be put into four broad categories: cultic/mythological, dramatic, allegorical/symbolic, and natural/literal.

Cultic/Mythological

This argument to interpret the Song of Solomon as mythological or cultic is by far the least popular of the four opinions. "According to this view, the poem does not really speak of human love at all; rather, *it is either the celebration of the sacred marriage of a goddess in the person of a priestess with the king, or else it is the celebration of the victory of the divine king over death and drought.*" This approach was originally put forth by self-proclaimed polytheists, and their opinions need to be understood in light of that presupposition. I only mention this position briefly because most evangelical scholarship today ignores it completely. The main three interpretations by scholars today are outlined below.

Dramatic

As we read the Song of Solomon, certainly there is a sense that what is unfolding before us in the text is a drama. After all, we see romance, love, desire, a "hero," and pursuit—all in a few short chapters as we watch these characters interact. But the term *drama* in this sense does not mean a "formal drama," synonymous with a "play" that was meant to be acted out on a stage, but rather a "literary form that simply means it is dramatic in nature." One commentator, when referring to the Song of Songs as a drama, clarifies by stating, "I do not use the term 'drama' necessarily to imply that the text is written for enactment by actors, whether in a royal court or worship. The Song of Songs clearly has a dramatic form, even if only as a romantic drama between two lovers."

Though it is difficult to argue the point that, by form, the Song of Songs is clearly dramatic, the interpretations that would fall into this view are those that state *the Song of Songs was nothing more than a drama or a play to be acted out.*

This position is not without its problems because "there has been no consistency in the development of this view. Absence of stage directions, lack of agreement on how many characters, or who said what, the lack of any clear signs of division into 'acts' or 'scenes,' and the fact that the dramatic form never really caught on in the East have prevented this approach from gaining any extensive support." Also, it is rightly pointed out that with regards to the form of a dramatic play, "there is no evidence that this kind of literature, apart from the Song, existed in Israel."

The book contains a dramatic story, with dramatic characters and other dramatic elements, but it does not appear to be intended to be read as a drama in the sense of having been prepared for actors and a stage. This position is generally rejected in evangelical scholarship today.

Allegorical/Symbolic

A strong case can be made (and has been made) that the best interpretation of this book is allegorical in nature. Kinlaw points out that "the oldest documented interpretation of the Song of Songs sees it as allegory. This position was well-established by the first century of the Christian era and has had a long and illustrious history in both Judaism and Christianity." Provan argues that "the allegorical reading of the Song of Songs is probably at least as old as the literal reading."

The allegorical approach essentially says that the book does not portray actual events rooted in history but is entirely a symbolic narrative. Some have seen it as a "parable glorifying human and divine love, an Israelite allegory teaching God's love for Israel, or a Christian allegory revealing His love for the Church." The Catholic Church at one point had even identified the bride in the Songs as the Virgin Mary.

Is it possible to read the text as an allegory? Can we see the book as a picture of the love of God for the Church? "The usual Christian interpretation given to this book is that it represents the love of Christ for His Church…According to this view, Solomon is a type of Christ and the Shulamite a type of the Church. However, the careful student of Scripture will realize that this cannot be the primary interpretation of the book since the Church was a secret hidden in God from the foundation of the world and not revealed until the apostles and the prophets of the New Testament (Rom. 16:25–26; Eph. 3:9)." It is difficult to take the primary interpretation of the book as allegorical love between Christ and the Church, as the Church would not be revealed for another thousand years.

Scores of other commentators concur and point out that it is oddly written if it is meant to be simply allegorical. "It is somewhat difficult to believe that an ancient Hebrew author, primarily intent on speaking on a relationship between God and God's people, would have composed the Song of Songs in precisely the way that he or she did, with such heavy emphasis on the erotic aspects of love and particular passages such as 8:5b–7, where the woman (i.e., on this reading, the people of God) takes the initiative in 'rousing' the man's (i.e., God's) love." In other words, the more *intimate* portions of the text can be somewhat symbolic, but why go into the details of the erotic love between the two, which obviously does not parallel the metaphor of Christ and the Church?

Great caution must be taken as one undertakes to study this book (or any other biblical text for that matter) as a solely symbolic allegory. "While the Song of Songs illustrates the deepening love we have with Christ, we must be careful not to turn the story into an allegory and make everything mean something. All things are possible to those who allegorize—and what they come up with is usually heretical. It's almost laughable to read some of the ancient commentaries (and their modern imitators) and see how interpreters have made Solomon say what they want him to say."

Since many ancient and contemporary evangelical scholars have seen this is in some sense a plausible interpretation, an allegorical approach must be given some consideration, though we must proceed down this road with great caution. I would offer that if someone wanted to teach on the love of God for his people to go to other texts (1 John 4:7–21, Rom. 8:35–39) that speak to that great truth explicitly. This method of interpretation can, at best, be secondary to a natural or literal interpretation.

Natural/Literal

This approach views the people as real and the events as literal. This is the natural way to understand the text, so if someone wants to take the book as other than literal, the burden is on them to make their case. So far, the cases against a literal approach fall far short. *The Nelson's New Illustrated Bible Commentary,* for example, starts out by simply claiming, "The Song of Solomon is a moving love story between a young country girl and King Solomon." These commentators assume right off the bat that the author is literally Solomon writing about an actual young woman.

> Whatever *application* this love story may have to God's relation to His people, or Christ's love for His church, it seems better to insist on a literal *interpretation* of this book for the following two basic reasons. First, it is inconsistent to allegorize this story and insist on taking the Gospels and other parts of Scripture literally. Second, taking it literally does not contradict any other teaching of Scripture. Rather, it complements it in many ways. God instituted marriage (Gen. 2:23–24). God created sex and gave it to humans to enjoy within the bonds of marriage (Gen. 1:27; Prov. 5:17–19). Paul declared that sex should be exercised within monogamous marriage (1 Cor. 7:1–5). Timothy was informed that sex within marriage should not be forbidden (1 Tim. 4:14) and that God 'gives us all richly all things to enjoy' (1 Tim. 6:17). The Song of Solomon is a beautiful example of real romance between two actual people that extols the biblical view of sex and marriage (emphasis his).

Conclusion

So it seems upon this research that the natural approach is the best way to read this book, if the four must be done exclusively of each other. So do the four approaches need to be exclusive of each other? If the best reading of the text is a literal approach, is any part of this text in any way an allegory or a picture of things that existed then (God and Israel) or things to come (God and the Church)? Perhaps there are two levels at which this needs to be read: literal (natural) and allegorical. It seems apparent that the natural approach is vital and primary, but "it is impossible to rule out allegory (or at least a second and deeper sense of the text) as one aspect of the text's intentionality."

It seems that the allegorical approach makes sense in some form but not as a primary method of interpretation, and certainly not as an exclusive one. Does an author have to only have one purpose in writing, especially when the author is ultimately divine? Is not the Holy Spirit wise enough to move a human to write a book that can be read on multiple levels? Provan again says, "An author need not have only one aim in writing or only one intention in the words they use. Why can the text not be assumed in its original intention to be both about human love and about divine-human love?" "The New Testament uses the same metaphor positively. Ephesians 5:22–33 teaches that the relationship between a man and his wife is analogous to the relationship between Jesus and the Church. The intimacy of marriage pictures the intimacy of God's love for us. Thus, it is not inappropriate to read the Song of Solomon as a poem reflecting on the relationship between God and His people, as long as the primary reference to human sexuality is not repressed." "While the primary reference is to human sexuality, the book does teach us about our relationship with God."

I therefore believe that the best way to understand the authorial intent of this book is to understand that it has some dramatic elements, but it is not intended to be acted out as a play. It has some allegorical elements that are to be taken very carefully and compared against the rest of Scripture to determine the soundness of the interpretation. "Without the literal sense as an anchor, it has always been too easy for men to sail the good ship of allegory wherever they wished, avoiding those things in the ocean that they did not wish to comprehend."

A literal reading of the love between a man and a woman seems to be the primary means of understanding this wonderful book of the sacred Scriptures, with room left for seeing the text as, secondarily, a picture of the love between God and Israel and/or Christ and the Church.

PURPOSE

The Song of Solomon is a profound story about love between a man and a woman. Today we need to hear this story repeatedly and let it soak in our souls and permeate our thoughts and actions with regards to love, sex, romance, and marriage. This book is an incredible "canonical corrective to the perversion of sexuality" that is prevalent in our society today. Our culture is driven by sex and relationships, and God in his goodness provided a moving story to give us an example of how it should work according to the Designer.

It is obvious from this book that sex does not make God blush. "While certain Jews and Christians have prudishly avoided the book as 'sensual,' some of the most devout saints throughout history have reveled in its pages." So should we.

Why so much sex-talk in the sacred Scriptures? "If the Bible is the book about God, then one may well ask what a narrative about human sexuality has to do with theology. This is an even more potent question when one notes that God is never mentioned in the entire text (except possibly in 8:6) nor are there any references to prayer, worship, or piety... To resolve this difficulty, it is important to remember that the Bible not only describes who God is and what God does; it also tells us what God desires for His people. The Song of Solomon provides an example of how God created male and female to live in happiness and fulfillment." If we want to truly live the Christian life to the fullest, we must have a deep understanding of how to live like a Christian with the opposite sex. The Song of Solomon is a marvelous text in the Scriptures to help us do that exact thing.

This book can move us in our faith and deepen our love for the Lord as well. "The major theme of this book is human love between a man and a woman. Many striking images communicate that this love is sensual, intimate, exclusive, and important. Since the broader canon describes our relationship with God as a marriage, the more we learn about married love, the more we also learn about our relationship with our divine spouse."

So, open this book. Study its truth, enjoy its precepts, and revel in the freedom found there. Most importantly, exalt the Creator to which it points us, and then proclaim the life it gives to the dying world, now more than ever.

BIBLIOGRAPHY

Alexander, David and Pat, ed. *Eerdman's Handbook to the Bible.*
Grand Rapids: William B. Eerdman's Publishing Company, 1983.

Dyer, Charles, and Eugene Merrill. *Nelson's Old Testament Survey.*
Nashville: Thomas Nelson, 2001.

Geisler, Norman, and Thomas Howe. *When Critics Ask: A Popular Handbook on Bible Difficulties.*
Grand Rapids: Baker Books, 1999.

Kinlaw, Dennis F. "Song of Songs." *In The Expositor's Bible Commentary,* ed.
Frank E. Gaebelein, vol. 5. 12 vols. Grand Rapids: Zondervan, 1991.

Longman III, Tremper. *Song of Songs.* Vol. 6. 18 vols. Cornerstone Biblical Commentary, ed. Philip
W. Comfort. Carol Stream, Il: Tyndale House Publishers, 2006.

Longman, Tremper III and Raymond B. Dillard. *An Introduction to the Old Testament.*
Grand Rapids: Zondervan, 2006.

MacDonald, WIlliam. *Believer's Bible Commentary.*
Edited by Art Farstad. Nashville: Thomas Nelson Publishers, 1995.

Provan, Iain. *The NIV Application Commentary, Ecclesiastes/Song of Songs.*
Grand Rapids: Zondervan, 2001.

Radmacher, Earl, Ronald B. Allen, and H. Wayne House, ed. *Nelson's New Illustrated Bible Commentary.* Nashville: Nelson, 1999.

Wiersbe, Warren W. *The Bible Exposition Commentary: Old Testament Wisdom and History.*
Colorado Springs: Victor, 2003.

Matt Chandler on Philippians

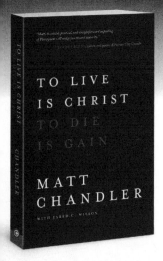

TO LIVE
IS CHRIST
TO DIE
IS GAIN

MATT
CHANDLER

WITH JARED C. WILSON

Using Paul's radical letter to the Philippians as his road map, Matt Chandler forsakes the trendy to invite readers into an authentic Christian maturity.

The short book of Philippians is one of the most quoted in the Bible yet Paul wrote it not for popular sound bites, but to paint a picture of mature Christian faith. While many give their lives to Jesus, few then go on to live a life of truly vibrant faith.

David C Cook
transforming lives together